Dear Big Folk

Welcome to Wee Deoch an' Doris!

This book re-imagines the lyrics of the song, **'Jist A Wee Deoch an' Doris'** to make it suitable for children. The song was written and performed by Sir Harry Lauder who lived from 1870 to 1950.

If you're not familiar with the tune of Harry's song, please go online and have a listen on YouTube or listen to us singing along on our Bletherin' Blog at **www.theweebookcompany.com.**

This book intends to give us all the opporchancity to sing together across the generations. What a happy way to keep Harry's abundant positive energy alive!

With love from

The Wee Book Folk

'Happiness is one of the few things in this world that doubles every time you share it with someone else.'

Sir Harry Lauder

It was the day of the Laird's birthday party. Lots of his pals had come to celebrate and wish him well, hale and hearty.

Above the grand front door of the big hoose, Wee Deoch an' Doris had cooried doon for a wee snooze.

Wee Deoch woke up and cried, 'Oh my! Is the party over?'

'Dearie me!' sighed Doris, **'did we fall asleep?** It's so quiet! There's not even a wee peep!'

Oh no!

It was the fairy friends' job to stay invisible and sprinkle and twinkle wee magical drops of love and light over everyone who visited the big hoose. It made everyone feel happy and bright! But this time they'd overslept! Had all the party guests left?

Oh no!

They took such pride in their secret fare-thee-well's! They made folk's hearts swell!

Sure enough, everyone at the big hoose party had let loose. **They'd had a hoolie!** In truth, things got a wee bit unruly but now the tomfoolery was over.

As the big clock chimed ten, everyone knew then it was time to go. The Laird and his pals had had a ball – sausage rolls, lollipops, birthday cake and all!

The guests had gone home. Although the party was fun, after it was done they felt that something didn't feel quite the same. **What a shame!** They were feeling a bit sombre and were starting to ponder ...

Fergus the ghillie was feeling down and a bit chilly!

Morag the builder was feeling flat. She was still wearing her boots and her hard hat.

Morven the pilot was sitting under her clocks, feeling sad that the party had stopped. 'How time flies,' she sighed.

Wee Deoch an' Doris flew into a flutter!

Wee Deoch started to mutter, 'oh no! oh no! We were a no-show! The guests have left! We didn't do our best! We didn't do our magic! Jings, it's just tragic!'

'Don't panic!' Doris cried, 'hang on! Maybe not everyone's gone!'

They flew to the window and took a look. The night was saved! Someone inside was saying 'cheerio!' to the Laird with a big cheery wave.

'That's great!' they cheered, 'it's not too late! Someone's still here!'

'Can you see? Can you see?' asked Wee Deoch.

'Who could it be? Who could it be?'

'Someone's saying bye bye!' answered Doris, 'oh aye!

I definitely spy someone with my little eye!'

‘Hurray!’ cried Doris, **‘it’s Harry!** We may have missed the rest of the guests but Harry’s the one that we love best!’

‘Woo hoo!’ cried Wee Deoch, ‘we know just what to do!’

‘Hurry! Make haste!’ cried Doris, ‘there’s no time to waste!’

Harry, the Laird’s best-est smiley-est pal was standing on the front step holding his hat and just like that, Wee Deoch an’ Doris zoomed into flight!

They started to invisibly sprinkle and twinkle a wee drop of magical golden fairy love and light.

Harry started to feel joy and wonder, as he caught a wee hint of tiny wee sprinkles and twinkles he seemed to be standing under.

With his eyes squeezed into tight wee wrinkles,
he tried to peer and see clear.

'What's that?' he asked himself, looking up from under his hat,
'is there something happening here?'

But he couldn't see.

'Wonder what it could be?' he sighed, all happy and peaceful
and starry-eyed.

Wee Deoch an' Doris fluttered and flew and sprinkled and twinkled all the while, in grand style.

And then they did their favourite thing – they started to sing their magical song in their tiny wee fairy voices ...

Jist a Wee Deoch an' Doris
Jist a wee drap tha's a'
Jist a Wee Deoch an' Doris
Before we gang awa'

Harry felt the energy of the special wee song touch his heart. He started to feel so full of joy, so full of glee, that he felt there was nowhere on earth he'd rather be!

As light as air, without a care, he suddenly jumped so high, **he felt he could fly!**

Wee Deoch an' Doris hugged and smiled.

'Job done!' the fairy friends cried.

They were as one. Spreading a wee drop of love and light with a wee song to help folk along before they went away, each and every day.

The friends sighed, stretched their wings and went back to their wee sleepy places with wee happy faces.

From above the front door, they gave out happiness galore. They just couldn't wish for more.

'Time for a wee snooze?'
asked Wee Deoch,
'time for a wee rest?'

'Aye, that's the time that I love best,' answered Doris.

In the twilight, in the gloaming, Wee Deoch an' Doris had done their roaming.

Through the still night, in the soft low moonlight, Harry went on to make his way home. He started to softly sing a song that came to him from deep in his heart ...

Jist a Wee Deoch an' Doris
Jist a wee drap tha's a'
Jist a Wee Deoch an' Doris
Before we gang awa'

More words of the song came back to Harry, who was disappearing gently into the darkness ...

There's a wee wifie waitin'
In a wee but an' ben
If ye can say it's a braw bicht moonlicht nicht
Ye're all richt, ye ken!

In the soft low moonlight
through the still silent night
Harry's song echoed
beyond the big hoose, over
the hills and far far away.

Harry's song went on to find its way to echo throughout the land forever and a day, and through the years, all the while, **it made everyone who ever heard it softly smile.**

WEE DEOCH AN' DORIS

by Susan Cohen
illustrated by Katomarans

www.theweebookcompany.com

A catalogue record of this book is available from the British Library

ISBN: 9781913237356

Printed in Scotland by Bell & Bain Ltd, Glasgow

THE WEE BOOK COMPANY
wee books with big voices

FSC
MIX
Paper from
responsible sources
FSC® C007785